Other Christmas books by Carol Ann Duffy

Mrs Scrooge

Another Night Before
Christmas

The Christmas Truce

Wenceslas

Bethlehem

Dorothy Wordsworth's
Christmas Birthday

The Wren-Boys

The King of Christmas

Pablo Picasso's Noël

Frost Fair

Christmas Poems

Advent Street

Christmas Eve at the Moon
Under Water

Three Wise Men

Carol Ann Duffy

Illustrated by Julia Klenovsky

PICADOR

First published 2024 by Picador
an imprint of Pan Macmillan
The Smithson, 6 Briset Street, London EC1M 5NR
EU representative: Macmillan Publishers Ireland Ltd, 1st Floor,
The Liffey Trust Centre, 117–126 Sheriff Street Upper, Dublin 1, D01 YC43
Associated companies throughout the world
www.panmacmillan.com

ISBN 978-1-5290-8395-8

Copyright © Carol Ann Duffy 2024
Illustrations copyright © Julia Klenovsky 2024

The right of Carol Ann Duffy to be identified as the author of this work has been
asserted by her in accordance with the Copyright, Designs and Patents Act 1988.

The right of Julia Klenovsky to be identified as the illustrator of this work has been
asserted by her in accordance with the Copyright, Designs and Patents Act 1988.

All rights reserved. No part of this publication may be reproduced, stored in a retrieval
system, or transmitted, in any form, or by any means (electronic, mechanical, photocopying,
recording or otherwise) without the prior written permission of the publisher.

Pan Macmillan does not have any control over, or any responsibility for,
any author or third-party websites referred to in or on this book.

1 3 5 7 9 8 6 4 2

A CIP catalogue record for this book is available from the British Library.

Printed and bound in Spain by Gráficas Estella

MIX
Paper | Supporting
responsible forestry
FSC www.fsc.org FSC® C116313

This book is sold subject to the condition that it shall not, by way of trade or otherwise,
be lent, hired out, or otherwise circulated without the publisher's prior consent in any form
of binding or cover other than that in which it is published and without a similar condition
including this condition being imposed on the subsequent purchaser.

Visit *www.picador.com* to read more about all our books and to buy them.
You will also find features, author interviews and news of any author events, and you
can sign up for e-newsletters so that you're always first to hear about our new releases.

For Adrienne

A Traveller was out on the road when the snow came down, so they made their way towards the light of an ancient Hall and banged on the door – once, twice, thrice – with the iron head of a lion.

It was the twelfth night of the winter feasts
and giant yule logs had burned without cease
since St. Stephen's Day. Pages hithered and thithered
with meat and mead, and the Traveller was welcomed

to take their ease if, being a stranger, they would judge
which one was true of three tales told
by three throned men whom three short straws
had appointed Wise. *Ascern by thine ears and eyes.*

The Traveller was a listening soul, who'd come to learn
that a lie was a bored truth; that fact
read fiction with envious eyes; that faith
would follow falsehood away to War. They settled down.

The first began: an enormous gent with a beard
like a spade, which seemed to shovel the air
as he spoke.

        MY STORY is true and concerns a shoe.

A sequence of dire events had fetched me up

swinging the cooking-pot my wife had thrown after me
when I left, as I limped into these parts – skint,
starved, shafted, screwed, strung-out, rattling, half-shoed –
where no one would help. Not one coin

clinked in my pot. Outside the alehouse, not one drop
was offered my way. I was moved along
from highway and byway – and not in a shy way.
Not one shop let me rummage its stinking bin.

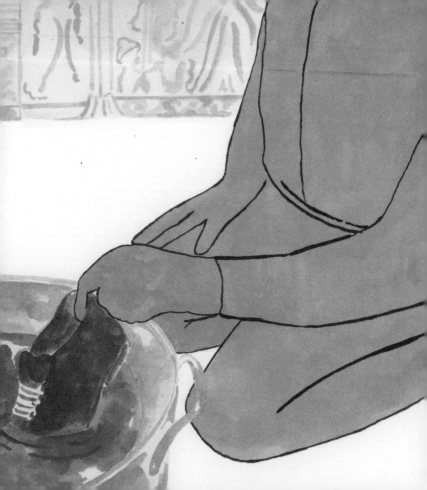

It is, dear Company, at times like these Invention
rolls up its sleeves. I filled and boiled my cooking-pot
by the Town Square stocks, and when a crowd
had gathered to jeer and boo, I tossed in my only shoe.

Fair to say, a silence fell (perhaps the smell?)
but then a Goodwife demanded What was my dish?
And being told Shoe Soup, bawled that it must be seasoned
with pepper and salt and chucked in a fistful of each.

Another's opinion was onion, so she pulled three
from the rope at her neck and juggled them in.
Word spread. Folk ran to their homes for carrots, parsnips,
turnips and spuds, celery, parsley, rosemary, thyme...

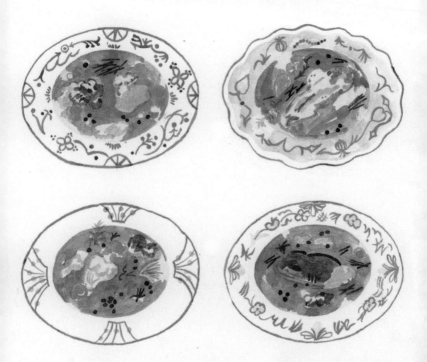

And more! A prize-winning marrow arrived in a barrow.
A blessing of lentils came from a nun. A butcher
prevented a dog from a juicy bone. I praised the Lord
and whistled and sang and adjusted to taste as I stirred.

Then they brought out their bowls and spoons, to share
in my soup, and when the final scrumptious drop was supped,
there at the base was a second shoe! Next thing I knew,

they rang out the bells and pronounced me Mayor.

Since when – high on the hog, revered – I've presided there.
If you need proof, look down at my mismatched shoes.
If you seek truth, then listen to no tall tales. It is he
who cannot savour the soup in an empty pot who fails.

16

The Traveller nodded and sipped at their mead, expressionless. They remembered times on the road when supper was sleep. A wretch could be hungry enough to stomach a lie, or to swallow their pride. But not tonight.

The second commenced: a beautiful youth
with auburn hair, who sniffed at a white rose
in a tapestry pose and perfectly balanced a bright tear
in each green eye.

I THOUGHT I would die

for Love, so I planned twelve Gifting days.
From my orchard, I dug up a pear tree
and replanted it, under cover of night, near the pond
in my sweetheart's garden. Twenty-three birds I trained,

to perch or roost, coo and cluck and call, sing
from the tree; to forage and peck, lay their double-yolk eggs
in the long grass; or swim on the pond in paired hearts –
all except one. So imagine my consternation,

passing hopefully by, to see my birds being plucked,
de-boned, rolled, trussed, stuffed, trimmed, even
the pretty partridge shoved up the arse of a goose —
and not one luminous pear remained to gild my tree.

But ardour burned in me. I would send her
not just a single ring, but five – five gold rings –
so with one she must marry me. I lurked at her gate,
heard only the mocking chorus of her and her mates.

I made a list of my friends and acquaintances.
I had forty-eight. I sent them round in a festive gang,
as to a wedding feast; clanking milk churns,
banging drums, leaping, prancing, piping, dancing.

Not one returned. I sat on an upturned pail – treeless,
fruitless, birdless, useless, ringless, friendless. Heartbreak
is endless. I spill two tears upon a rose. What's true is true
is true. If you make a song of this, I'll sue you.

The youth had a point, for some of the Company
had started to holler *Five Go-old Rings!*
and a flushed Page called for a comfort break.
The Traveller stepped outside. No footprints puzzled the snow.

And so to the last of the three Wise men:
a bony cove with a beak for a nose and flinty eyes;
a voice like a loud whisper, older than Time.

THE NIGHT I died, they had laid me to sleep

in the upper room, from where I could still hear
the comings-and-goings below. My wife was crying;
my mother praying; her sisters cooking; and men
in the garden outside, smoking and talking quietly.

It was all very pleasant. I could smell tobacco
and rising bread and fatted calf. Sometimes,
a brief laugh fluttered at the door like a moth.
Where is my soul, I thought, to get this done?

I was excited to die. To me it was Win-Win.
If there was nothing, I'd never know. If there was something,
I would begin. And I had a secret of sorts –
I was tired of life. I had loved Peace,

yet they taxed me for distant wars. I had valued Truth,
yet they tallied my vote for lies. History
was a charlatan. Myself, irrelevant. I fixed my gaze
on the old stone in the sky and started to die.

And I'm here to tell you I did. Three days and nights
I lay cold in my winding-sheet. So I was unaware of pounding feet
on the stairs; the lowering down of my bed
from the roof; the lamentation and grief; until

in a messy, flailing, roaring rush, like a birth,
I gasped alive. I recall the sharp sparkle of blood in my veins;
then food and wine among the olive trees;
the miracle-man smiling under the lamps.

I have little else of interest to say, except
to wonder – if you believe me, why? For me,
the world did not change. As you see, I have still not died,
though I swear to you all, before God, I have tried.

A toast was proposed to the three Wise men
and round went the Wassail cup. The younger knights
were rowdily placing bets – which yarn was feasible, believable,
fake or true, nonsense or preposterous or credible.

A goshawk flew to the rafters, clutching a mouse.
The Traveller stood on their chair, raising a hand,
then declared in a clear, loud voice which tale was true.

Reader, they chose the selfsame one as you.

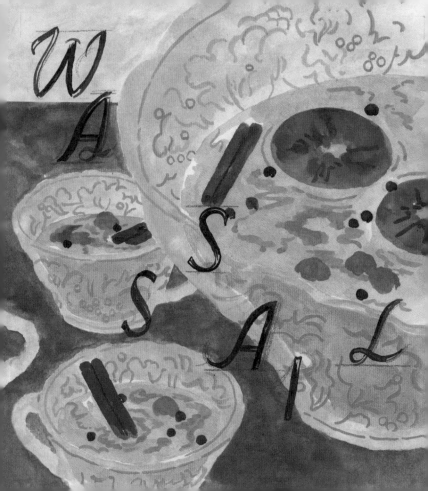

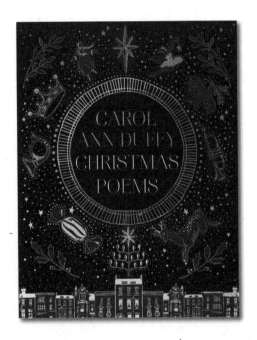